UnPack It
8 Steps to Effective Bible Study

Contact Information:
Pilgrimage Educational Resources
1362 Fords Pond Rd, Clarks Summit, PA 18411
570.504.1463
simplyapilgrim.com
ontrackdevotions.com

UnPack It: 8 Steps to Effective Bible Study

Published by:
Pilgrimage Educational Resources
1362 Fords Pond Rd, Clarks Summit, PA 18411
www.simplyapilgrim.com

Printed in the United States of America

Copyright © 2011 Pilgrimage Educational Resources, Clarks Summit, PA
Visit our website: simplyapilgrim.com

All rights reserved. No part of this publication may be reproduced, stored in a retrieval system, or transmitted in any form or by any means - for example, electronic, photocopy, recording - without the prior written permission of the publisher. The only exception is brief quotations in printed reviews.

Any internet addresses, email addresses, phone numbers and physical addresses in this book are accurate at the time of publication. They are provided as a resource. Pilgrimage Educational Resources does not endorse them or vouch for their content or permanence.

Author: Dwight E. Peterson
Executive Developer: Benjamin J. Wilhite
Contributing Editors: Joshua Wilhite, Joshua Jones, Don Chapin, Wade Yocum
Graphic Design: Lance Young (higherrockcreative.com)

ISBN-13 978-0692255315
ISBN 0692255311

10 9 8 7 6 5 4 3 2 1

How to Use This Resource

Unpack It was written and designed with two purposes in mind. First, we want to show you how important Bible study skills are for the spiritual lives of your students. In fact, these skills are absolutely vital to the long-range success of your ministry. Second, we want to help you evaluate the present condition of your ministry as it relates to teaching Bible study skills. From there we will help you build a strategy to deliver Bible study skills to your students

Unpack It is divided into two sections. The first section will show you how to build Bible study skill in your own life and in your ministry. Each chapter ends with key questions that can be used for personal evaluation, for small groups, or for ministry team training. The second section is a curriculum outline for teaching individuals or groups how to build the skill of effective Bible study. It is set up as four lesson plans. Each lesson covers two of the eight steps outlined in this resource. Each lesson plan is followed by corresponding student worksheets.

Ideally, a ministry team will walk through this resource together to evaluate their own ministry approach and build a strategy for investing in the Bible study skill of those they lead. That strategy may include the use of the tools offered in this resource, tools designed by the ministry team itself, or any number of great tools available from our ministry and others. The important thing is that you build a strategy and implement it. It's an investment that will not return void!

While this resource is written from a local church ministry perspective, the same principles can be applied by parents, mentors, para-church ministry teams, or average folks who just want to grow.

Reality Check

I remember as a young youth pastor, being discouraged because of what appeared to be a lack of real spiritual growth in our young people. As a youth pastor, I was committed to our students having daily Bible study—so much so that I made sure that there were always devotional guides available for my teens. I made a point to regularly let them know that I had provided those resources and strongly encouraged each teen to use them. I was really committed to it. Most of the students were not.

As I sat in my office one day, I wrote down all the behaviors that I knew were necessary for somebody to grow spiritually and walk with God. Then I asked myself a question that completely transformed my ministry: "Where am I actually training young people at this church to do those things?" My answer was: "Nowhere."

Honest evaluation pointed to the reality that we were not highly committed to skill development. Discipleship was merely the transfer of information. It was about getting students to accept a body of truth. If they could identify that truth and know it, then I considered them spiritual. In fact, follow up was similar. If a student trusted Christ, we immediately got them involved in basic Bible-doctrine classes with a traditional classroom or teaching format. What we didn't do was teach our students the skills necessary for spiritual growth.

Students did not know how to have daily devotions. How could I expect them to dive into Scripture, let alone find success with it, if they didn't know how? On top of that, their parents didn't know how to have devotions either - unless they were like my father. He was committed to it and figured out how to do it by sheer will power. Unfortunately, that was not the norm.

My dad was a businessman. He grew up in the church and was an active member. One day, my dad evaluated his walk with God and concluded that he was lacking passion. He just wasn't experiencing intimacy with God. After concluding he was tired of apathy, he figured out what was his most profitable hour of the day. He committed that hour to spending time with God. He told his secretary he was not to be disturbed for that one hour. He didn't really know what he was doing. My dad just opened his Bible and prayed. That was the beginning of significant change.

One thing that changed his family of four boys was his decision that we were all going to have our devotions every day—not together as a family—but as individuals. We were all required to read our Bibles each day. We had to use a notebook to record the date, the passage we read and anything we got out of it. We had to leave our notebooks out where he could check them. And he did...religiously. My dad kept his own notebook that we had the freedom to check. He never missed a day.

My father traveled, so it was normal for him to be gone a week at a time. When he came home, he retrieved each of our notebooks. In our home, no place was off limits to my parents. My dad's philosophy was, "It's my dresser, it's my bed, it's my room—I'm just letting you use it for awhile." After checking my notebook he would say, "Dwight, I noticed you're three days behind." He didn't have to say anything else. I understood that it meant, "Get to your room and don't come out until you're caught up." That's just the way it was.

I've spent over three decades in local church ministry, teaching ministry and educating future ministry leaders through academics, coaching and mentoring. In all that time it has become clear to me that modern ministry is primarily content-based. Pastors, teachers, parents, recording artists, authors, counselors and most others tend to process Biblical truth and package it for quick consumption. Modern technology makes this content readily available in a dizzying array of formats that are readily accessible. It's a flood of biblical proportions. This is not inherently a bad thing. God specifically gifted members of His body with teaching gifts that are designed by Him to build people up.

However, this content-focused phenomenon is producing a dangerous result that is screaming for our attention. If all the content is already processed, how and when does an individual believer learn the skills necessary to process it on his own? Is it okay to outsource the process of daily Bible study, to the "professionals?" What if instead we could balance content with foundational Bible study skills? What if those skills would allow our churches and their members, old and young, to follow the example of the Bereans and search the Scripture for themselves? Can we help believers become "self-feeders?"

I hope that, on some level, you have already crossed this bridge. No doubt some have already seen this problem and developed some strategies to train people to study God's Word for themselves. However, if you ask the question I did as a young youth pastor, "Where am I teaching people at this church these skills?", and your answer is "Nowhere!," keep reading. The eight steps outlined in the following pages will give you a solid start toward a worthy investment.

Key Questions

1. As a young believer, what methods were used to train you in the development of your relationship with God?

2. In your current leadership roles (ministry, parenting, etc...), what methods do you use to train others in the development of their relationships with God?

3. How would you assess the level of success of your students as it relates to a growing personal relationship with God?

4. How would you assess your own personal relationship with God?

5. What do you think are the key factors in an intimate growing relationship with God?

6. What are you doing to train yourself and those you lead in the skills necessary to succeed in each of those factors?

Part 1

Eight Steps

Remember that part of any skill development is frustration. I still become frustrated with my skill level and frustrated in the process of developing skills. Stick to it. Helping students, parents and leaders understand this process will not be easy. No skill development process is.
-Dwight

Step #1
Skill vs. Content

Rewind to that day in my office when my moment of clarity happened. That day, I realized something crucial. If you evaluated the way I was "doing church" as a youth pastor, you would come to a scary conclusion. My actions showed that I believed the only thing a student needed to do for spiritual growth was listen to someone teach what the Bible says. What was Sunday school? I taught Bible. What was the Sunday morning service? Someone taught the Bible. What was Sunday night service? Someone taught the Bible. And at youth group, I taught the Bible. At our socials and other activities I could be found teaching the Bible. Is that a bad thing? Not necessarily. But it was completely one-dimensional and my students' entire youth group related exposure to the Bible was filtered through me.

The first step in helping someone learn the skill and discipline of personal devotions is to understand the difference between skill and content. Content is, essentially, the conclusion a reader draws about what the text says. Content-focused curriculum or tools present the conclusions the writer has come to about what the text says. This approach is the proverbial "give a man a fish." It only feeds him today.

Skill, on the other hand, is the ability to figure out what the text is saying and to understand how that message should play out in the life of the reader. The goal of skill-based curriculum is to grow the user's ability to handle the content of the text directly, to evaluate it correctly, and to connect its relevance to his life. This approach is the proverbial "teach a man to fish." It feeds him for a lifetime.

I realized that if I taught my students what the book of James says, I had taught them only what the book of James says! This is not to discount the value of knowing what James says. We need to teach the Scriptures to all people at every level of understanding and take advantage of the opportunities the teaching role gives us.

The Scriptures are powerful and the ministry of the Holy Spirit is powerful. If I can teach a person basic skills, if they have the right approach to studying the Bible, and if they have the Holy Spirit living inside of them, they can come to a proper understanding of the Word of God. We just have to teach them how.

As a pastor, I concluded that I had done two things wrong. First, I had failed to help students understand why these skills were so vital. Second, I failed to teach them how to develop these skills.

Understand that we are talking about teaching a skill, not teaching a conclusion. That may sound like semantics, but it isn't. The goal is to teach an effective method to figure out the meaning of the content for themselves, not to teach them the actual content. The skill is permanent and lasts a lifetime. The content is limited to what you can teach in the time you are given. Later we'll deal with providing students with a tool. We'll work through a tool designed to teach them a skill, as opposed to a tool designed to deliver content.

Realize too that skill-based teaching is a process. Development will take time and effort. There will be natural cycles of success and failure. Coaching is vital and it's not a spectator sport. It will often test the patience and perseverance of both the teacher and the student. At the same time, some students will excel along the learning curve more quickly than others.

To drive the point home, let's imagine an average junior high basketball camp. The first thing we notice on day one is the obvious developmental differences among the campers. Some look like they should still be in elementary school. It takes the full force of their body to get a regulation ball from the free throw line to anywhere within the air space of the basket.

Then there are the blessed few that have the size, coordination, and talent to start on the Junior Varsity squad. Most campers fall somewhere in the middle of these extremes. Many have played in junior leagues. Several have not. Where do you begin? What will it take to prepare each camper for basketball success? Showing game film of the district champion high school team, Pistol Pete Maravich's shooting form, or the movie Hoosiers will do something to tip their minds toward what it will take to be successful in basketball. Having the star player from the local high school basketball team model textbook free throw shooting form is probably helpful. But in the end, real development comes from handling the ball, drills, repetition, scrimmages, and game experience.

Did you grow up in a church or a home in which you were given the message that personal devotions were a key factor in your spiritual development? In your home or in your church, were you taught a specific method of how to have devotions? Were you provided with a tool to be able to use that method? Were you given a system and an opportunity to practice and hone your skills? Were you provided with accountability to stay on track with that skill? In most cases, the answer to those questions is a resounding "no."

Each year a professor of a college freshman class asks me to come in for a day to talk about this issue of devotions. It's amazing to me what happens when I present that list of questions to an average class of one hundred Bible college students. Only five or so kids will raise their hands. Yet all of them come to our Bible college "ready" to be trained for vocational ministry leadership. We are supposed to train them for ministry leadership, and these students don't know how to have devotions.

This story often ends in tragedy. Kids may grow spiritually because they are in a solid church and come from a solid home. At Bible college, they may grow spiritually because they take Bible classes and attend daily chapel. They graduate, accept a pastoral position, and begin to design their ministry strategies around programs and processes, just like they were taught to do. But they struggle with engaging the Word of God personally because they haven't developed the skill and discipline of effective, daily, personal Bible study. What they have learned is technical, not personal in a spiritually life-transforming way.

In our youth ministry, we decided that on Wednesday nights, youth group would no longer be about listening to me. We were going to teach kids how to have personal devotions. It changed everything.

We also decided that in addition to our new routine on Wednesday nights, our goals and the way we measured success would be based on skill development areas. When a student trusted Christ, our first priority was developing his core skills, not pumping him with content. So, we began by getting him a Bible, teaching him how to read it and developing his ability to interpret and apply it. Students would often say things like, "You know, I keep seeing the word baptism in here. What is that?" We responded with, "Let's take five or six weeks, study this and figure out what it is." We wanted students to learn how to have devotions, read the Bible, and pray.

There are eight important steps we will cover in teaching students the skill of personal devotions. We just covered step one. "Learn the difference between skill and content development." Please understand that I am not saying there are eight steps students must take each time they have personal devotions. But if you are going to teach students the skill and discipline of personal devotions, then you must follow these eight steps. In the next chapter, we will cover step two.

Key Questions

1. If someone else looked at how you do ministry, what would they say you believe is necessary to help people grow?

2. Are you more content oriented or skill oriented? How did you determine your answer?

3. What are you presently doing in each of those areas?

4. What skills are you effectively training your students to perform?

5. How can you reorganize your ministry to become more balanced between content delivery and skill development?

6. How will you prioritize the skills you will begin to teach?

Step #2
Build Investigators

About the same time I was sitting in my office as a young youth pastor making a list of the things necessary for students to grow spiritually, *Living by the Book*, by Howard Hendricks, hit the market. I devoured the book and committed myself to teach students how to study the Bible using his method. When I served as youth pastor in Elkhart, Indiana, we actually devoted the entire 9th grade Bible class in our Christian school to learning Bible study methods using Hendricks' book as the foundation. We developed it into a curriculum to teach students how to study the Bible.

In Hendricks' book, he teaches that the first Bible study skill is observation. That means learning how to be an investigator, not a record-keeper. Understanding and teaching that difference is key to this whole process. Most of our training and most of our devotional guides are what I would describe as recording keeping Bible study. Devotionals typically prompt the reader to answer questions like, "Who was Jesus talking to in verse 4? What did Jesus say in verse 3?" Those questions prompt a response that is similar to fill-in-the-blank questions. I call that record keeping. It is similar to methods used in schools. We read to acquire facts to recite for a test. Then we pretty much forget everything we read.

What if your students learned to be investigators instead of record-keepers? What if instead of filling in blanks, they asked effective questions? What if instead of acquiring information about a passage, they understood the passage?

To help make this transition for our students, our leadership team got together on Wednesday nights to talk about the kind of questions our students could come up with. I practiced with our leaders by asking them to read a verse and come up with three questions that begin with the word "how." Another time I might ask for three questions that begin with "could" or "why." I wanted them to learn how to begin the process of digging into Scripture to find what was there. I wanted them to approach it with a curious mind. If our leaders could get it, they could model it for our students and become an effective part of the training process.

The Scriptures are amazing to me. I've been studying them for over four decades and the more I study, the more I discover how much I don't know. That realization motivates me to dive in and find more. The Bible is incredible, but when we make Bible study about record keeping, it can be just the opposite. Reading a passage of Scripture and writing down the facts pales in comparison to reading a passage and investigating all that it contains.

I am currently involved in the youth group of a church plant. On Wednesday nights I often have the students read a passage of scripture and then ask what types of questions someone could come up with from those verses? Then I might ask, "As you read, what questions come to your mind?" They might run into a vocabulary issue and wonder what is meant by this word? Recently, we were in 2 Peter and one of the students asked a few questions. "Who is Balaam? Why is a donkey talking? What is that all about?" These types of questions get to the heart of the passage. It was so much better than just asking students who was mentioned in verse 15.

Questions like, "Who? What? Where? When? Why? What if...? How did...? When did...? Why did..?" are foundational to building skilled investigators. They may be questions that can't readily be answered, but they feed the discovery process. They create a need to find answers. They drive us to further study and even better questions. They take us beyond record keeping to really discovering truth.

God gave me a wife who was designed to help me with this. I appreciate this now, but early in our marriage it created strife. When we were first married, I decided that I needed to have devotions with my wife. So we tried it, and the process drove me out of my mind. Bonnie would say things like, "You know what? I wonder what Mary's aunt thought when she found out that Mary was pregnant?" My response was, "First of all, Mary's aunt isn't in the text. Nobody really cares what Mary's aunt thought. Further, why are we going to talk about abstract things that make no difference? Let's get back to what we're supposed to be doing." Ultimately, I decided that she should have her own devotions, I should have my devotions, and then at supper we could talk about it. I realized later that Bonnie thought of something interesting by asking what appeared to be abstract questions. Even if the answers were not readily apparent, the questions flowed from and fed her genuine curiosity for what was really happening in the text. They added a sort of 3-dimensional aspect to the discovery process that was not just interesting, but was vital.

Consider the passage in Matthew 26:6-13, where Mary anointed Jesus' feet with oil. What questions could you ask that go beyond basic record keeping? Try these on for size. How did Jesus respond? Who was at the dinner? Why was the dinner being given? Which Mary was this? There are many Marys in the Bible. Is she the prostitute, Lazaraus' sister, or another Mary? Would Jesus' mother anoint her son with oil? That would change the story, wouldn't it? Why did she choose this method to express her love? How much was the perfume worth? Why did the people at the dinner respond this way?

These are just a few. How many questions could be asked of this text? Hundreds? Thousands? No matter how many times you have engaged a specific passage of Scripture a new question will help you see it with new eyes. This is especially true when your questions are born out of a current situation in your life. As one of my seminary professors used to say, "Read it again for the first time."

A while back I was studying Psalm 139 with some college students on the Appalachian Trail. I chose this passage because I heard a series of messages looking at the four attributes of God that David described. I thought that would be a great study on the trail. But while I was hiking God didn't use the attributes to speak to me. It was David's statements in verses 23 and 24. "Search me, O God, and know my heart. Try me." David wanted to be right with God. "Would you please examine me?" I wondered what it was about David's understanding of those four attributes that led him, when he fully comprehended them, to go before God and say, "Please, I want to be vulnerable. Please just search me and know me."

God knows everything perfectly. What does omniscience have to do with coming to that point in your life? He is everywhere fully present. How will a deeper understanding of omnipresence cause me to want to be more and more vulnerable before my God?   How is it that having a fuller understanding of who God is causes me to want more and more vulnerability in my life? How would it lead to less self-protection, less defensiveness?   How would it make me say, not only to God, but to others, "Would you please look at my life, because I want to be right." Do you know how many times I've studied and taught that text and never asked those questions?

As we talked around the fire one night, a student defined omniscience as God knowing everything about everything. She said, "You know, it hit me today when I was thinking about omniscience that He knows everything about me, and in spite that, He still died on the cross for me and loves me."

I thought to myself, who wouldn't want to go to that kind of person and say, "Would you look at me and see if there's any wicked way in me?" I'd never thought of that before. My thoughts about omniscience previously revolved around how He knows everything about the things external to me. But after thinking on this, I realized that whatever I did and whenever I did it, He was there and saw it. Did you ever do anything and hope that no one saw, or would find out? He already knows, so what would be the point of self-protection in your communication with God? Why be defensive instead of allowing Him to look deep into your life and reveal to you what He sees?

Good questions are powerful.   They move people from ignorance to understanding by the very fact that they require answers. Good questions are not fill-in-the-blank record keeping questions. They yearn for a deeper understanding of the text and how it connects with the reality of the reader's life today. If we are going to teach students to develop the skill and discipline of daily Bible reading, we must teach them to ask good questions.

Key Questions

1. How can you more effectively teach kids to investigate the text instead of becoming record keepers?

2. How can you provide opportunities for kids to practice and interact with this skill?

3. In what ways do your present teaching methods and devotional guides help or hurt the development of this skill?

4. How can you do a better job in your programming of teaching your students how to develop the skill of observation?

Connect the Dots...

This step is key. No short cuts or cutting corners on this one. It's one thing to ask quality questions that beg for answers. It is another to find the answers to those questions. Gaining the skill and experience to find the answers can be one of the more difficult hurdles in the process of Bible study. Connecting the dots is a learned skill. If we are going to help students build the skill and discipline of effective daily Bible study, we must go beyond helping them become investigators and teach them how to develop their interpretation skills.

I was once invited to participate with a senior English class at one of the local public schools as the youth pastor of a "Baptist" church. They had just completed reading the book, "Paradise Lost," and the teacher spent the following week having a representative of different religions come in and answer any question the students had. On the day I attended the class, I began by writing "The cat is red" on the board. I led them in a brief discussion about what this might mean.

We discussed possible meanings for the word cat or the word red. Students enjoyed coming up with crazy suggestions. One student guessed the sentence was saying that a really cool dude was a communist.

I ended by asking them if they would agree that there are many correct interpretations to that sentence. The obvious answer is that there are many "possible" interpretations, but not many "correct." I then asked them how they might determine what the correct interpretation was.

They asked questions like, "In what context was the statement written?" Was it spoken in a parking lot at the Caterpillar plant in Iowa or at a news conference at the local animal shelter?

They asked questions like, "What did it mean to those who heard it?" Did they laugh? Did they gasp? Did they start an ad campaign against dying animal fur different colors? They naturally come up with the kind of questions we need to ask when attempting to find answers to the questions we are creating in our investigation.

For instance, think about one of the questions we asked in the last section. "Why did Mary choose the time, place and method she did to express her love for Jesus?" Knowing the background of the situation is crucial in understanding why Mary did what she did, when she did it, and the way she did it. We need to do research to gain information about the original context so we can more fully understand it in ours.

Think about a passage like John 10. Christ illustrated how much God loves us by comparing Him to a shepherd who loves his sheep. For children of that day, it would make perfect sense. They would walk away amazed that God would love them like a shepherd loves his sheep. But to students today, it makes little or no sense unless we help them understand the love of a shepherd in that culture.

Another key tool for interpreting the Word is the Word itself. There are often other passages that speak to a specific point in a passage of Scripture. This is particularly helpful when evaluating vocabulary words. Are there other passages that use this same vocabulary word you are studying? Are there other passages which give details about the story I am reading?

Why was the dinner given? What makes this passage so significant is the answer to that question. While Matthew does not tell us, John's account in chapter 12 tells us it was given to honor Jesus.

Going back to Matthew 26, how would we find out who is at the dinner? Do we get everybody's name here in Matthew? Where else could we go to find out who is at the dinner? In this case, the other gospels (Mark, John) contain parallel passages that round out the picture.

And who is at this dinner? The disciples, Lazarus, and a man identified as Simon the leper. Whose home is the dinner at? Why is it important that it's at the home of Simon the leper, and that he is the host of the banquet? It may appear obvious, but going back to the questions above, why is that significant? It is significant because if Simon the leper is at his house eating dinner with guests, we can also deduce that calling him Simon the leper was incorrect. We must now call him "Simon the ex-leper". If he were still a leper, he would not be near his home, but would have been put out of his house and town because of this disease.

So we have Simon the ex-leper, the disciples, and Lazarus, who was raised from the dead. Knowing why this banquet is being given and who attended adds unbelievable significance to what happens at that meeting.

How much was the perfume worth? It was worth one year's wages. When you teach this passage, it's helpful to pick different vocations and list their average salaries for context. If you used Bill Gates, the perfume was worth $150 million or billion or whatever. If you use a social worker, maybe it was worth $22,000. Maybe have each student pick an adult they know and assign what they think that adult's annual salary is to the value of the perfume. In any case, it would take a year of Mary's life to replace the value she poured out.

So why did the people at the dinner respond the way they did? What was their response when Mary anointed Him? How can you be Simon the ex-leper and watch this take place and possibly use the word "waste?"

When I first started thinking about this, I thought, "Surely, I don't understand what the word "waste" means." The text says, "Why this waste?" I thought it must be one of those Greek translation issues and maybe they were really saying, "Why didn't she do this publicly? Why did she anoint him before us, who understand? The world needs to see this!" But when you study the Greek word translated "waste," you see the reality is worse.

How did Jesus respond? Do you think that question is important in understanding this text? In fact, what we're doing right now is exactly what Jesus said would happen. He said, "You guys have it so wrong. Your response is upside down. This moment and what this woman has done is so significant that people will talk about it forever." Here we are, two-thousand years later, talking about what this woman did in that place and at that time.

Do you see how to help students do with the Scriptures what they would naturally do with a sentence like, "The cat is red?" Consider how different this approach is from the record-keeping method of Bible study. Imagine the excitement and enthusiasm it generates to bring the reality of a passage off of a black and white page and into living color. All we're doing is asking deeper questions and painting in the answers as you find them.

At the beginning of this section, I said this is one of the more difficult hurdles for skill development. It's the most likely point in the process where students will disconnect and give up. Why? In short, until they have some experience and coaching, they will spin their wheels on how to find the answers. They may quickly develop the skill to ask good questions, but action steps like cross-referencing Scripture, finding historical context clues, and doing word studies are big challenges to the uninitiated.

So what can you do to deal with those challenges? First, be proactive. Know the challenges are coming and be ready for them. Gather whatever resources you can make available to students for their personal time and show them how and where to use them. Resources may include concordances, lexicons, and other traditional Bible study tools. Keep in mind that all of these require a little training to use properly. There are several online versions of these resources that vary in quality, but they may be more accessible to students during their personal study time. Even helping a student purchase a solid study Bible could be a simple step in the process.

Another good suggestion is to encourage students to write down the questions they have and the walls they bump into. They can record these in their Bible study journal or devotional book. Have them bring those questions to their small group, their mentor, their parents, or even a peer that is ahead of them in the learning process. The key here is to give them both hope and anticipation that there are answers. They will find answers and, in the process they will learn how and where to find them on their own. Ideally, you will be able to tie this search process and the resources back into the spiritual relationships the student already has. That will more effectively build their spiritual development around the Word of God.

This is also where your own teaching and preaching can be helpful. When you teach, take the time to demonstrate how you came up with the answers to your own questions. Let them in on your own struggles so they realize that this skill is challenging to us all, but that with hard work we get it.

David told his son Solomon in Proverbs 1 and 2, that Biblical truth is out there for us all. God has not hidden it in some code we can't figure out. It does take work., though For those who are willing to dig in and find answers, the Word of God will explode. But in a good way. Have fun!

Key Questions

1. What are you presently doing to help students develop their interpretation skills?

2. How can you more effectively teach students to develop proper interpretation skills?

3. What opportunities and resources can you provide to your students to practice and interact with this skill?

4. In what ways do your present teaching methods and devotional guides help or hurt the development of this skill?

5. How can you do a better job in your programming of teaching your students how to develop the skill of interpretation?

Step #4
Put Skin On It

Once the dots are connected, it's time to begin connecting concept to reality. What does it look like in skin? What does it look like in your skin... not someone else's? In particular, it is critical to begin injecting Biblical conclusions into the real situations of real life. The traditional term for this step is application. What's the point of this whole process, if it doesn't result in real change in real lives?

A few years ago I attended a Conference hosted by a church in West Michigan. The main speaker was Jerry Bridges. I was asked to also speak at the conference in a workshop for youth workers. In one of his main sessions, he said something profound relating to this next step. He said, "The Bible was not written to increase your knowledge, but to guide your conduct." In that brief statement, he captured what I had thought and tried to say for many years. The point of Bible study is not knowing content, but knowing how it will change my life.

Presently, I teach at a Bible College. One of the challenges of teaching there - or at any level - is helping students become motivated to learn what is being taught. What prevents them from being passionate about my subject, or any other subject for that matter, is a failure to see the importance of its content. Our youngest son often asked us while attending high school why he had to take a particular subject. He would often ask, "When will I ever use this stuff in real life?" Or when he was feeling particularly spiritual he would ask, "When am I ever going to use this as a youth pastor?"

This question reveals the biggest flaw in education. We have never answered or even given the freedom to ask, "SO WHAT?" In other words, "What difference does this make? I feel so strongly about this that I write that question on the board in all of my classes. I tell my students that if they ever wonder why we are talking about this, or why I am giving this assignment, just raise a hand and ask, "SO WHAT?" I think we often interpret that blank look as apathy. What if it is really the inability of students to connect what they are hearing to real life? We are thrilled about what we are teaching or discovering, and yet they couldn't care less. We must help them connect what they are learning to real life situations they face. We must give permission to always ask, "SO WHAT?"

Peter told us, "His divine power has given us everything we need for life and godliness through our knowledge of Him." Everything we need is in the Bible. We just need to learn how to take the truth we discover and connect it to our lives. We must never teach a truth without helping people answer the "so what" question in their own minds.

There are two primary challenges to the skill of application. The first hurdle is helping students draw the connection between the principles they dig out of Scripture and their own life situations. In reality, what we face here is a cross-cultural or translation issue. The solution presents itself as we train students in the prior step. The more they learn proper interpretation skills, the more they will be able to get over this hurdle.

We must helps students learn to see the original readers and the characters in the Bible as real flesh-and-blood people with real life situations, problems, trials, victories and emotions. What we read actually happened to real people.

The second challenge is drawing clear parallels to their own life situations. The Bible is always relevant because it was and is written for real people. A principle we see in a text was never meant to simply stand alone as an intellectual truth that amazes us. It was intended to be a truth that touches our personal lives. We must always ask the question, "SO WHAT?"

As a pastor, parent, teacher, or mentor, your primary tool here is modeling. Often a well-focused question followed by a personal "for-instance" will do the trick. Let me explain.

Jump back to the Matthew 26 example. What are possible applications in this passage? What if after the hard work of doing proper interpretation we asked ourselves the question, "SO WHAT?" Mary anointed Jesus with perfume that was worth a year's wages. "SO WHAT?"

Among others, an application could include honoring Jesus with our lives and possessions. We could ask questions like: What have you ever sacrificed? Have you ever been so moved by love and appreciation for what God has done in your life that you responded extravagantly?

Another application might be recognizing that God can and will respond to the honor given Him exceedingly abundantly above what we can ask or think.

Think about the comparison between what Mary gives Jesus and what Jesus gives to her. While a major focus of the passage is the cost of the perfume in a human sense - Mary's economic sacrifice - the comparative value of what Jesus gave her in the eternal honor in Scripture might draw a different picture. He is the Rewarder of those who diligently seek Him (Heb. 11:6).

What if the key application here is God's extravagance as it relates to our own? How does that connect to the "right now" of your students? How does that answer the "SO WHAT" question? How would that play out for you and your students right now?

Think also about applications that might come from the reactions of others at the dinner. They responded with "common sense." How does Jesus' response to them reveal His view of their positions? How might this relate to a situation at school or at work in which a believer honors God publicly and gets some type of negative response from peers, authority figures, or whomever?

What about application to our personal lives? What have you given to Jesus to express how much you appreciate what Christ has done for you? Have you given your time to invest in church ministry or in the lives of people around you? How much money have you given to church or missions or to simply help someone in need? When I teach this to my students I don't use Bill Gates as an example. I use a college kid that makes $1200 a year. What can you present to God as an "I did this simply because I wanted to show you how much I love you" gesture? It might just be getting up each morning to have your devotions even when you are exhausted from a late night youth event or a late shift at work.

Here's an example from my life. There are two places on this earth that I despise. One is a fabric store (a story for another day). The other is a grocery store. There are times I'll go to the grocery store (very few I must admit) and spend over an hour there with my wife. When I walk next to her with a positive attitude my presence communicates to her that I love her. She knows I hate the grocery store. She also knows there could be only one reason why I am there. I love her. Dearly.

Let's look at a different angle. As a pastor, one of my greatest joys was seeing a student realize God's call in his life to full time vocational ministry, whether on the mission field, in education, or in pastoral ministry. There were several times when the parents reacted to that calling with, "What a waste? Why would you want to do that when you could be a doctor or a lawyer? You have a brilliant mind."   Does that sound like any attitudes from the Matthew 26 passage?

We are simply helping students learn to verbalize their questions and responses. Often those responses have been ignored or stifled since early childhood. "WHY?" "SO WHAT?"

A final point to remember in teaching this step is the impact one's spiritual maturity has on one's ability to make application. Let me explain.

According to Hebrews 5:11-16, there are two types of Biblical truth. The writer of Hebrews refers to them as milk and meat. At first glance, it might appear that milk and meat refer to Biblical truth that is simple or difficult to understand. A closer look into this passage reveals that it is far more than that.

We learn in this text that milk is Biblical truth that simply requires an intellectual ability to accept. The writer of Hebrews refers to a number of subjects when identifying those items which he lists in the milk category. Meat, however, is truth that impacts how we live. The writer of Hebrews refers to them as "the teachings about righteousness."

Meat is exactly what we have been talking about here. Spiritually mature people are those "who by constant use have trained themselves to distinguish between good and evil." It is milk when we can interpret what Jesus said when he spoke about turning the other cheek. It is meat when we begin to talk about how that truth impacts my conduct at school or work. Spiritually immature people usually have a hard time gaining this skill. But if they do not, they will not mature!!!

At the end of the day, this skill step is about helping students translate what they learn in Scripture into a solid understanding of what it looks like in their own skin. Once they have that down, you can help them put the rubber on the road. That's next.

Key Questions

1. How free do the students in your ministry feel to ask the "so what" question?

2.   What are you intentionally or unintentionally doing to encourage or discourage students to ask that question?

3. How can you more effectively teach kids to apply what they are correctly interpreting to their personal lives?

4. How can you provide opportunity for kids to practice and interact with this skill?

5.   In what ways do your present teaching methods and devotional guides help or hurt the development of this skill?

Step #5
Rubber... Meet Road

When is a liar no longer a liar? When he stops lying? According to Scripture, it is when he starts telling the truth. When does a thief stop being a thief? When he stops stealing? According to Scripture it's when he stops using his hands to take from others and starts helping others instead. Why is that question important to our understanding of this next step? To explain, let's think about two passages of Scripture.

First, in James 1:22-25, James talks to us about two kinds of responses to the Scriptures. He writes about hearers and doers. In this text he warns us about simply being a hearer. His concern is that, as a hearer, we will deceive ourselves. Why is he so concerned about this? The answer is in the text.

A hearer is described as someone who looks at himself in a mirror. When he does this, he sees himself as he really is. He is the person who goes beyond interpretation to application. In other words, a hearer is someone who has taken the important step of determining how a particular principle applies to his life. This is the student who can verbalize what he learned in his devotions and how it applies to his relationships at home. But, he is deceived into believing he is spiritually mature because he only sees himself in light of what the Scriptures teach. He walks away from this revelation and does nothing to change it. He remains the same and continues to behave the way he did before understanding how the principles applied to his life.

The doer is one who can't forget what he discovers and goes beyond application to implementation. He sees himself as he really is and is determined to put a plan into place to change in light of what he saw. He understands how disrespectful he is to his parents and wants to change his behavior to that which pleases God. He sees his need to be victorious over sin in an area of his life and is determined to be successful.

My own story is peppered with the results of an anger problem. When I was newly married, one of my fears was knowing there was a real possibility I might, under the influence of anger, hit my wife or say something so unkind I'd never recover from it. By God's grace neither of those things ever happened. I do remember in the first year of our marriage, being so angry about something that I almost lost control. I saw something in my wife's eyes that absolutely destroyed me. It was fear. In that moment I had two thoughts. One was that I would never, ever, ever, cause that look again. Whatever I had to do, my wife would never be afraid because of me. The other thought I had was about her dad, the man who gave his daughter to me. He entrusted her care to me. I determined I would never again respond to his daughter in a way that would disappoint him. That was over 30 years ago. One of the motivations that motivates me to be in the Scriptures even today is the idea of the man I would become without the refining power of God in my life. Acknowledging you have an anger problem is not the same thing as doing something about your anger problem.

As I mentioned before, the Bible was not written to simply increase our knowledge. It was written to guide our conduct. We need to create a plan to integrate our Bible reading into our lives. We have to make it a reality.

It is vital to help students learn how truth applies to their lives. But we are also responsible to teach them how to implement that truth into their lives so it changes the way they think and act. They must move beyond being a hearer of the Word to becoming a doer. They desperately need our help to do that. We must also help them develop a specific personal growth plan that targets the areas they want to see change. It might include building accountability into their lives. Students need people who will keep them accountable and pray with them as they work to see those changes take place. It goes beyond realizing their thought lives are out of control, or that they do not honor their parents as they should. They need to actually see change in those areas.

This is why true Christian fellowship is so important. God never intended us to take this journey alone. Accountability and small groups can be so effective in the development of life application skills. Good accountability is not simply checking to make sure your students are having personal devotions. It pushes them to follow through on what they learned. Imagine what would happen if loving people asked your students specific questions about what they were trying to apply to their lives?

So again, making a decision is great. Realizing how a principle of Scripture ought to impact my life is great. Actually changing is even better. Implementation is always the ultimate goal.

Key Questions

1. How well do your students apply Biblical truth into their lives?

2. What are you doing within your ministry to help students learn and follow through with this skill?

3. How can you better teach kids to develop strategies to implement their learning into their lives?

4. What kinds of opportunities can you provide for your students to practice and interact with this skill?

5. In what ways do your present teaching methods, devotional guides, and programming help or hurt the development of this skill?

Step #6
Provide a Tool

Let's pause before we take a look at this next step. It is vital that we continue to keep in mind where every step we have taken so far is designed to lead us. Our goal is not simply to help students learn the skill and discipline of daily Bible reading. Our goal is to help students learn the skill and discipline of "effective" daily Bible reading. Ultimately, daily Bible reading needs to change the way students live.

So, the point of this next step is not to find a tool that will just get students to read their Bibles every day. The point is to find a tool that also helps you teach students the step between regular Bible reading and life change. The tool you choose needs to help accomplish this ultimate goal. Let me illustrate.

I recently spoke with one of my good friends. I called him because I had previously called his wife in order to "check up" on him. He lives in Florida and has been on many wilderness trips with us. He left every wilderness trip admitting what a lousy husband he was and identifying the areas of his life that needed to change. Guess what he did for the next year. He continued to be a lousy husband.

For six years he learned what he should do, but never got over the hurdle to actually do it. One summer the lid came off of the problems in their marriage. Soon after that my wife and I ran into them with their youth group at a Teen Leadership Conference. Bonnie and I took the opportunity to spend some time with them. I called her four months later and asked how things were going. She started to cry and she said to me, "I've never been more in love with my husband than I am right now! What's happened in his life is a miracle. It's unbelievable."

I called him to let him know about the conversation I just had with his wife. He said to me, "You know, all these years I knew it, I knew it, I knew it. One day I just decided that I was a fraud. I went on those wilderness trips and sat around the fire and cried. I would tell the guys how hurt I was that I wasn't the kind of dad or husband I should've been. They would gather around and hug me and I would go home the same guy I was before the trip."

I am sure you can imagine the joy in my heart to see a life and marriage changed through God's power. Tragically, this doesn't often happen in our churches. Imagine the change we could see if students were trained to take that vital step of application. So again, your next step is to find and provide a tool that works with the Bible study method you're teaching. It needs to help students learn to implement their learning into their lives.

As I mentioned earlier, years ago I concluded I had to reorganize our programming to better teach students the skills they needed to grow spiritually. After reading "Living by the Book," I determined that this Bible Study method would be the foundation for teaching our students how to study their Bibles. Once I made that decision, I began the search for a tool that would help us with this skill.

I soon discovered three realities about the tools we came across. First, some guides gave students great insight into the passage they read, but the assigned Bible reading was not enough. They required only a verse or two of random selections of Scripture. Second, I found guides with more Scripture, but the devotional thoughts were not helpful to the students. They didn't reinforce the method I was teaching them. Third, none of the guides seemed to help students progressively learn the skill of effective daily Bible reading. They might model the skill, but didn't help students develop it for themselves. I found the guides I looked at were "content based" and not the "skill development" type of tools we were looking for.

I decided to create a new guide which would have as its primary goal the teaching of the skill and discipline of effective daily Bible reading. I wanted it to work for different age groups and different levels of spiritual development. I did not want it to just teach what the Bible says. I wanted to enable students to develop their own skill of determining what the Bible says. The result was "OnTrack."

Again, whatever tool you choose, make sure it is one which not only reinforces a Bible study method but also allows the them to develop their own Bible study and implementation skills.

Key Questions

1.   How effective are the tools your current Bible study tools, in teaching your students the skill of "effective" daily Bible reading?

2.   What is it about those tools that make them effective or ineffective at teaching the skills you are working to develop in your students?

3.   Do you need to provide a more effective tool or help students become more effective using the tools you presently have?

4.   What steps need to be taken in light of the answers given above?

Step #7
Create Opportunities

Now things really get moving. You need to provide students with opportunities to practice the method and share the results of their own personal daily Bible reading. That is, give them some way to actually use what they're being taught and regular times for them to share the results of their study.

That's exactly what we started doing on Wednesday nights. In fact, our purpose statement for Wednesday night was "to train students to develop the skills that will enable them to grow spiritually." On the nights we worked on the skill of effective daily Bible reading, we met in our small groups. We began the conversation by asking what was learned in the past week from their personal Bible reading. What questions were asked? What were the answers or applications for the questions asked? I found this time with students to be encouraging for me personally. I would often discover more about what a passage says from their responses. Listening to other people's insights deepens everyones' learning. Often a student's question would send my mind in a direction I never thought about before.

A few years ago, our church had a night of skiing at a local mountain in town. Bonnie and I both grew up skiing, although it had been a long time and our children had never gone before. I had three methods to choose from to teach my children to ski. First, I could just take them to the mountain, provide the skis, and tell them to have fun. Would they learn how to ski that way? Eventually they would. Second, I could find books or videos about skiing. I could make them watch the videos and read the books and then take them skiing. Would they learn how to ski that way? The answer would again be "yes." Third, I could take them to the beginners slope, and take a few hours to show them how to ski by doing it with them, one step at a time. As a parent, which one would you choose? As a child, which would you choose? It's a no-brainer.

Why would I choose the third option if they can learn to ski with either of those other methods? The other methods are like teaching children not to touch the oven. You could allow them to burn their hands on a hot oven and they would learn what you want them to know. But that's a very costly lesson. I'm not willing to pay that price. Are you?

While we understand how to teach skills like skiing or not touching a hot oven, we don't often translate what we know about skill development into the church setting. A common reason is the time involved. The priority of our weekly youth programming is usually to teach our students what we think the Bible says.

What might happen if you really took the time to have regularly scheduled "devotions practice?" What if that choice resulted in your students actually developing the skill and discipline of effective daily Bible reading?

I became so committed to this that at our Junior High and Freshman summer camps we eliminated the morning Bible hour and replaced it with "devotions practice." Students sat with leaders and counselors and did devotions together each morning. The results were amazing.

I sat with the Freshmen each morning and we went through it step by step together. They were learning how to use the tool they would be using during the entire school year. We walked through our devotions and practiced together.

Any skill we develop comes as a result of practice and use. Developing the skill and discipline of effective daily Bible reading is no different. To help our students develop the skill and discipline of effective daily Bible reading, we must create opportunities for them to practice the skill, and share what they are learning.

Key Questions

1. How are you providing students the opportunity to practice the skills you are teaching them?

2. In what ways have you provided your students the opportunity to share the results of the skills they are developing?

3. What do you need to do in order to provide a more effective practice time to help students productively use the tool you presently have?

4. What steps can you take to provide an effective sharing time for your students?

5. In what ways do your present teaching methods and programming help or hurt the development of this skill?

Step #8
Accountability Matters

We are finally at our last step of teaching students the skill
and discipline of effective daily devotions. At this point
you need to provide accountability. Students need support
and encouragement to stay on task. Accountability is also a
valuable tool to help assess their skill development. It keeps
you aware of how they are doing. It can also give you insight
on how to provide what is needed for continued growth and
development.

This was so important to our ministry that we made our small
groups about accountability. We believe in the building
of relationships within the body so strongly that we made it
foundational to what we did. In Hebrews 3:12-13, we are told
that we need to encourage one another daily. It is vital to
avoiding an unbelieving heart that ultimately turns away from
God. Authentic fellowship is essential for each of us to grow in
our walks with God and avoid sin.

Everyone in a small group was challenged to care enough
about the other members to ask how things were going
in their lives. We actively asked about and prayed for the
specific areas people were working to develop. We worked
to communicate the idea that everyone's spiritual walk was
all of our concern. Each of us needed to be involved in the
lives of others enough to help them along on their journey. If
they needed a pat on the back, we would provide it. If they
needed a kick in the pants, we would provide that too.

In addition to those groups, we put students together in smaller
accountability groups. They worked through a set of specific
questions each person would ask and answer. Many of the
youth leaders led one of those groups. For a number of years
I met with five guys on Tuesday mornings at 6:30 a.m. I began
with 10th graders and stayed with them until graduation.

We developed what we called "Tag 5" groups. These were
short, entry level accountability groups. They met for 5 minutes
each week to pray for each other. I got the idea from a Doug

Fields book, "The Purpose Driven Youth Ministry ." From there, the groups would often grow into more intimate and deeper accountability groups.

God never intended us to function alone. Think about the significance of the fact that we were created in the image of God. At the heart of God's image is the Trinity. Consider how Christ functioned with the help of the other members of the Trinity in His earthy ministry. If Christ didn't go it alone, how could we expect to?

If we are created in God's image, we are likewise created as relational beings. We must learn to build relationships with others in the Body of Christ. We need people who can help us stay on course and develop important growth skills. Creating an environment like this is key to whether or not students will follow through with developing the growth skills they will need in the years beyond high school. We must help students understand their need for accountability and then help them follow through to make it happen.

Key Questions

1. What are you doing now to create accountability for the people you minister to?

2. What steps can you take to move your group towards greater commitment to accountability?

3. In what ways do your present teaching methods and programming help or hurt the development of this skill?

4. What do you need to do to be able to help your students establish productive accountability?

Wrapping Up: Now What?

Let me close with what I hope will be some words of encouragement. First, I hope you do not see this material as a commercial for a particular tool. While I believe in OnTrack as a tool, these eight steps apply regardless of what tool you chose to use.

We became so committed to developing this skill in the lives of our students that we purposefully searched to find a tool we could use. We couldn't find one that met the needs we were after. We couldn't find one that we felt was truly committed at its core to teach students a skill and not simply provide content. So we created our own.

OnTrack is built on a three-year cycle. We discovered that it takes about that long to build a good foundation. In this cycle, a student can read through each New Testament book twice and read Old Testament books in each of the major time periods. They read Genesis through Deuteronomy the first year, the Kings era the second year and the Prophets the third year.

For each day, OnTrack provides a passage of Scripture and a devotional thought. That thought is written to help the student see how a specific study skill was used. Each day reinforces the development of solid Bible skills.

Remember that part of any skill development is frustration. I still become frustrated with my skill level and frustrated in the process of developing skills. Stick to it. Helping students, parents and leaders understand this process will not be easy. No skill development process is.

Finally, in the struggle to develop these skills, you will very likely run into Satanic opposition. He understands the impact this will have in people's lives. You can expect he will target you and your students to ensure they do not continue to develop these skills. Stay the course. Commit the battle to the One who has already won it.

Part 2
Teaching Bible Study

Christians need to learn how to read the Bible for themselves. They should be able to learn what God expects of their lives by listening to God's voice as it flows from the Scripture they read. The church, youth group, or parent that focuses exclusively on content will feed a student a spiritual fish. A church, youth group, or parent that teaches a student how to do their own devotions will feed them spiritually for a lifetime.
-Dwight

Curriculum Overview

Problem: Most churches and youth groups invest most of their time communicating the content of the Bible without teaching people to become skillful at searching the Word for truth on their own.   Churched children grow up with spiritual realities and perspectives dependent on parents, teachers, and pastors, if not media and other sources of input.

Goal: Christians need to learn how to read the Bible for themselves. They should be able to learn what God expects of their lives by listening to God's voice as it flows from the Scripture they read. The church, youth group, or parent that focuses exclusively on content will feed a student a spiritual fish. A church, youth group, or parent that teaches a student how to do their own devotions will feed them spiritually for a lifetime.

Objective: The student will be able to independently read, evaluate, and apply a portion of Scripture to his own life.

Process: This curriculum has been designed to be presented in four lessons.   Each lesson covers two of the eight steps. This material can be tailored to fit various circumstances. Based on the goal of this instruction, the instructor should provide opportunity for the learner to work on the process independently after a time of focused instruction.   The instructor should evaluate the learner's progress based on the process not the content.

Lesson 1

Step 1: Understand Skill vs. Content

Instead of teaching your people the "What" of Scripture, start by teaching them the "How" of Scripture. There are two general mistakes that are often made in teaching Bible study skills. The first is pressuring them to do it, but failing to give them good instruction. The second failing to model the skills in the instruction process. You need to show your students that they need to know how to spend meaningful time in the Bible with the intent of learning how God wants them to live his life.

The following questions are designed to help learners understand that the accumulation of knowledge is not the goal. The goal is to learn skills to study Scripture and find what God has for them there.

Use these questions as starters to the conversation. You may decide to send the questions home with students, then gather them at a later time to discuss their answers.

Discussion Questions:

Is the Christian life a journey or a destination?

If it is a destination, what should our attitude be towards learning the Bible?

If it is a journey, what should our attitude be towards learning the Bible?

When most Sunday school and youth group teachers present the Bible, are they building your knowledge of the Bible or your skill in learning the Bible?

Step 2: Be an Investigator...

Many systems for teaching Bible study gear students toward record keeping, not investigation.   Investigators start with questions. Teach your youth how to ask good questions. You (and they) will be amazed at the array of deep questions students will come up with when they bring a little curiosity to their Bible study.

Choose a passage of scripture that is not overly complex such as Matthew 26:6-13. If you are already using a devotional tool such as OnTrack Devotions, choose that day's passage. Have the students read the passage quietly, and then begin asking questions. Guide them away from frivolous and silly questions, but do not discourage serious questions that may stray from accepted norms.

Start with the traditional Who/What/Where/When/Why/How questions. Then move into the second and third generation questions that will naturally spawn from the first set. Avoid tossing rhetorical questions (the kind you already have an answer for) into the mix. Pretend you are reading it for the first time with no context whatsoever.

Sample Questions for Matthew 26:6-13:

Who attended the dinner?

Why was the dinner given?

Which Mary was this? Why did she care so much?

Why did she choose that way to express her love?

How much was the perfume worth?

Why did the disciples respond the way they did?

How did Jesus respond? Why?

Lesson 2

Step 3: Connect the Dots

The technical term is interpretation. What answers can we actually find to the questions we asked in Step 2? Where can we find them? What do we know about the passage in terms of the history, background, and context in which it is set? It's time for some brain work.

While the observation skills you began developing in the previous step require more development, the jump to interpretation is often the disconnect point for early skill developers. Why? It helps to have some background. As a pastor, teacher, parent or mentor, you have an opportunity here to set yourself up as a resource. You're not there to give answers. You need to operate as more of a compass than a commentary. Help your student learn what resources are available to connect the dots.

Resources may include reading the surrounding context, a good commentary, Google, or (after they have tried other resources) you. Ideally the resource will point the student back to Scripture that answers the question, or generates better questions.

A good resource will tell us that the Matthew 26 event is also shared in other Gospels (John 12, Mark 14).

Discussion Questions:

What other passages can help me understand this better?

How can/would I find passages to cross-reference my questions?

What do the other Gospel accounts tell me that I don't see in Matthew 26?

Step 4: Put Skin on It

What does this look like in skin? More specifically, what does it look like in your skin? The connection between the context of the passage and the learner is a vital bridge. Students have to come to accurate conclusions about what the passage has to say concerning their lives. This is the step that makes the passage come alive. Help them understand that these are not just fairy tales, but real events revealing vital lessons that God has written to help them live their lives.

A student needs to come to a clear perspective on how to apply that passage to life right now. A powerful question to answer is, "What does God expect of me?"

Stick with the passage(s) you began working through in the previous steps.

Sample Questions for Matthew 26:6-13:

Do I respond to God the way Mary responded to Jesus? Why or why not?

How do I respond to those around me that are "radical" in their expression of love for God?

Is my response more like Jesus' or more like the disciples'?

What/who do my actions and responses tell me that I value most?

What is the most expensive (money, value, or priority) thing I could pour on Jesus? Am I willing to do it publicly? Am I willing to get down on my knees and adore Him?

What is the most dangerous thing I could do to express my love for Christ and His love for others?

Lesson 3

Step 5: Put Rubber to Road

James 1:22-25 instructs us to be doers not hearers only. When teaching about Bible study, many instructors stop at the application level. Connecting the truth to personal experience is vital, but it is wasted if no practical plan of action is put in place to implement the application. Jerry Bridges said, "The Bible was not written to increase your knowledge, but to guide your conduct."

The goal of this lesson is to help the learner create a plan to integrate the learning into his life. The plan should be very practical, realistic and measurable. In other words, the best strategies are ones that have obvious steps that can be seen in action by those around you.

Using the discussion questions below, challenge your students to commit to at least one measurable action that flows out of an application they made in the last step.

The challenge for you is to be transparent and model it for them.

Discussion Points:

Pick one key application from the previous lesson and identify how it will look if you were to commit to it over the next week.

Are you willing to commit to it?

How will you know whether you are successful? How will you know if you are not successful? Write down at least one clear way you can measure success for each.

How will those around you know if you are successful? How will others around you know if you are not successful? Write down at least one clear way others can measure your success for each.

Step 6: Tool Time

This lesson requires more homework for you than for your students...at least up front. You need to help your students acquire and evaluate tools that will help them find success in regular daily Bible study. Pick one or both of the methods listed below to do this.

Method 1: Find Resources for Them
Find one or more tools that will give the students a skill-based framework for daily Bible study. A tool we build just for this is OnTrack Devotions. It's available at www.ontrackdevotions. com. It's important to get the tool into students' hands AND to orient them in how to effectively use it. Ideally the tool will challenge the student to walk through the process of observing, interpreting, applying, and implementing rather than just feeding them conclusions. Remember, the objective is not to tie their Bible study up with a tidy little package, but to stretch them to become self-feeders. Don't give them a tool that chews their food and digests it for them!

Method 2: Have Them Find Resources
The objective of this method is to instill evaluation skills in each student. This can happen as they decide what tools to use and how the tools will grow their capacity to do skill-based Bible study. In the days and weeks leading up to this lesson, ask each student to find a Bible study tool that they like...one that "works" for them. It may be one they are already using. It may be a journal they already keep on their own. It may be something they grab off the shelf or access online. Whatever the case, give them the responsibility to show up with a tool in hand.

During your teaching time, have each student, or several volunteers, share their tool with the group. Have them explain how it is structured. Ask them to identify where and how their tool walks them through the process of observation, interpretation, application, and implementation. Where there are gaps in that process across different tools, help the students build a strategy for how they will fill those gaps as they use their selected tool.

Lesson 4

Step 7: Create Opportunities

Most people will not follow through without commitment and encouragement. Help each student set a definite time and place that they will commit to doing their devotions. It will likely take some sacrifice. Here is a big question to ask. "Is a deeper relationship with their King worth the sacrifice of some time?"

In addition to creating opportunities, think also along the lines of helping students IDENTIFY opportunities to grow in applying their skill for Bible study. The questions below will help lead your discussion toward a well-rounded strategy that includes individual personal Bible study, community or group Bible study and the identification of other opportunities to stretch and grow Bible study skills.

Discussion Questions:

What time of day does your mind engage most effectively... morning or evening?

How often each week will you commit to doing personal Bible study? What days and times will you do it?

Are there any small group or church-related Bible studies you can/will join?

List all of the situations that may/will happen in a normal week in which you will be sitting in front of an open Bible. Include church, school, family or any other situations.

For each situation listed above, how will you invest the skills you have learned to make those times most valuable?

Step 8: Accountability Matters

With accountability, think three-dimensionally. Ideally, this topic will help your students identify both mentors and peers as accountability partners. They may even identify those they are investing in.

Accountability should be aimed at both the regularity of the student's Bible study and their skill development. While we know the Word of God will not return void, we also know it's vital for each student to grow in their capacity to dig into it, digest it, and apply it.

One great idea is to encourage students to commit to investing what they are learning with someone else as a mentor, teacher, or just as a friend. That can be a little scary for many students, but it is highly effective. There is a high degree of accountability that flows from a sense of responsibility. It may not work for every student, but helping them identify where they can invest their newfound Bible study skill and its application to their life is a worthy target.

Discussion Questions:

List at least one mentor and one friend in your life to whom you would be willing to be accountable for your personal Bible study.

How often will you meet with each of the people listed above to check in on both the regularity of and the quality of your personal Bible study time?

How will they know whether you are just "punching the clock" or whether you are actually growing? Give specific examples.

Are there tools or "check points" you can put in place to give them a regular window into your growth process whether you initiate it or not?

Who could you mentor, to help them grow in their Bible study skill? How can you relate that to what you are learning in your personal Bible study?

o✝d
ontrack devotions

www.ingramcontent.com/pod-product-compliance
Lightning Source LLC
Chambersburg PA
CBHW060541030426
42337CB00021B/4374